I WANT TO BE A
CHEF

Written by
Jonathan Reule

Illustration
Carlos Varejão

Storyboard
Christiane Tee

UNIBINO
BOOKS

First paperback edition August 2023
ISBN 978-981-17320-7-2

Published by Unibino Pte. Ltd.
31 Rochester Drive Level 3, #03-47 Singapore 138637

www.unibino.com

Food can be a source of joy and satisfaction for many. Eating a nice meal not only keeps our bellies full but can also make us happy for a time. Yet, if we come across a bad-tasting meal or consume food that makes us sick, then we become the opposite of a satisfied customer, and our food soon turns into a source of misery.

That's why we cherish skilled chefs in our modern world so that our eating experiences can be joyful instead of filled with grief. It takes more than just skill to make great dishes, though. Being a chef requires passion and a deep understanding of flavours and ingredients. If you're into cooking, baking, and preparing food in general, then you might make a great chef one day!

But perhaps our story begins over two million years ago when mankind first learned how to cook food over a fire. Before that, we likely subsisted on uncooked meals such as fruits, tubers, and vegetables, leaving a whole host of edible foods untouched.

What drove us to cook that first meal over a fire, though? It might've been done out of pure curiosity. It's possible we tossed a potato into some open flames and let it bake, only to find that after the fire had died down, we had a tasty meal waiting for us in the coals.

It didn't take long for this trend to catch on among ancient humans. For one, our tastebuds were naturally inclined to appreciate these new flavours, and secondly, by cooking food, we created more options for us to choose from. Unlike in our modern world, where we live with an abundance of food, back then, getting a daily meal could sometimes be a struggle.

That's why we decided to be creative in how we heated our food. Instead of putting meals directly onto fires, we began laying flat rocks over fires, making ancient frying pans to cook more delicate meals without burning them. We also learned that setting a pot of water over a fire would cause the liquid inside to boil. This gave us even more variety in what we could eat, especially when cooking grains, such as rice or durum wheat.

Yet, when did our meals and cooking methods become more complex? We don't know that for sure, but we do have some archaeological records from past civilisations that can give us some clues. Take the ancient city of Pompeii, for example.

Excavations of the ash-covered city have shown us that the Romans built functional kitchens, with several pots and pans and even furnace ovens to cook with. Although we don't know the exact dishes they made, we do know they made cuisines that incorporated a variety of ingredients, meaning these were potentially the first unofficial chefs to exist!

Although, every great chef needs great ingredients to make their dishes stand out, which is why we started to try other herbs and spices to flavour our foods. This new way of cooking took off like wildfire, and soon spices and herbs were being regularly traded throughout the world.

This was especially true in the East, where spices were highly valued and traded along the silk road and other maritime routes. Soon these ingredients were finding their way all across the world. In fact, for centuries, these spices were in such high demand that they became more valuable than gold at one point!

As we progressed into the middle ages, the art of cooking turned into a full-time position for many talented chefs. Kings, Emperors, Sultans and other powerful rulers employed cooks to oversee the preparation of large banquet meals and any last-minute requests made throughout the day or night.

The art of cooking became one of the utmost importance in those times when several famous cooks went on to write some of the earliest recorded cookbooks. This was an interesting step forward for cooks around the world. Having a standardised recipe allowed others to try out these dishes and make their own changes where they deemed necessary!

As we came into more modern times, there were bakeries, restaurants, cafes, and diners found in most major cities and towns spread across the globe. But the word Chef wasn't an official term for these cooks until the 1800s when they were used in French restaurants to help denote the different roles and titles among the workers in the kitchens. Did you know that chef actually means chief in French?

The title of Chef de Cuisine translates to the chief of the kitchen, or better understood as the head of the kitchen. This word stayed localised to France for some time until the first celebrity chef Marie-Antoine Carême became an international hit, travelling to various countries and cooking for people of nobility while making a name for himself and French cuisine.

It wasn't long after this that the word Chef became adopted by most of the world. This was also a time when these kitchen hierarchies became standardised. It was known that the chef wearing the largest hat was often the highest ranking in the kitchen.

Soon cooking schools were created to teach young aspiring chefs how to handle a kitchen and use the right flavours and techniques when making dishes.

The first cooking school in the world opened in 1879, the Boston Cooking School. But one of the most prestigious and longest-lasting schools opened a few years later, in 1895 in Paris called Le Cordon Bleu, where they trained chefs in the culinary arts, and still do to this day!

Learning all of this information may have you wondering what it's like to be a chef in this modern world. Well, chefs have lots of responsibilities when it comes to preparing meals for an entire restaurant full of patrons. They need to make sure that the food they are preparing is of the best quality before even starting to cook.

They should also make certain that their kitchens are clean, along with all the utensils and cookware they intend to use. Beyond that, they have a job to ensure that every dish they make is of the highest quality before being served to customers. That includes following recipes closely, making sure the portion size is correct, and being certain they follow any special requests from patrons.

Chefs are often on their feet the entire day while in the kitchen. They can be found running back and forth between stoves, ovens, mixers, and the service bar, ensuring that customers receive exactly what they ordered and in a fair amount of time. Many chefs also spend their days in heated environments, maybe over a hot stove or a brick fire oven, where they need to be able to handle the daily heat.

Whereas other chefs may need to ready themselves for a cold environment, especially if they are required to cut up chunks of meat or fish inside a chilled freezer. As you can see, being a chef can put you up against both extremes, from hot to cold. But another thing chefs need to be prepared for is the possibility of getting dirty on their job. From spills to messy flours, chefs need to be willing to take a few stains on their uniforms along the way.

You might be wondering now what it takes to be a chef. There are a few different paths to consider for this career. A popular choice is to attend a culinary school. At these culinary schools, you can learn from master chefs who will help train you to either open your own restaurant or to help you stand out from other applicants at a well-established business.

Another great opportunity would be to find a restaurant looking to hire junior-level chefs and learn on the job. This is one of the fastest ways to improve your skills and techniques while learning how kitchens really function in the world.

Why don't we take a look now at the different types of chefs and what roles are expected from them? Normally the entry-level chef in a restaurant is called the Commis-Chef, which translates to the assistant chef in French. The commis chef can be tasked with a variety of duties, from cleaning pots and pans to cracking eggs, washing and chopping vegetables, and even doing a bit of light cooking.

Next, there is Chef de Partie, which means station chefs who are in charge of a certain type of cuisine within the restaurant. For example, there are Saucier chefs who are in charge of sautéing dishes and preparing any sauces that may be needed in the restaurant.

Another example is a Pâtissier chef who will be in charge of all the desserts and pastries made within the restaurant. There are also Boucher chefs who work with meats and other butchery items, along with an Entremetier who deals with vegetables, soups, and starches if required.

The Sous Chef is second in command, often found working in a kitchen, overseeing all the operations while cooking many of the dishes, directing the staff and ensuring that food is delivered to customers on time.

They also make sure that the dishes are plated properly and that the kitchen continues to run smoothly during their shift.

Chef de Cuisine or sometimes called the head chef, is in charge of designing a restaurant's menu, coming up with how items will be plated, along with standardising recipes. These chefs can also be tasked with purchasing bulk orders of ingredients along with managing sales costs and daily expenses.

Finally, there is the executive chef, who oversees the entire operation of the restaurant. These chefs are often removed from working within the kitchen on a daily basis but instead will manage at a higher level and potentially manage more than one restaurant at a time. These professionals ensure the business is operating efficiently and earning enough to keep the doors open.

After this, you may be encouraged to be a chef yourself one day. Know that this job requires plenty of work and time dedicated to cooking in order to succeed. But if it's what you enjoy and feel passionate about, then your future can be bright in this field.

We will always appreciate chefs and their hard work for as long as we have eager tastebuds and hungry bellies. Who knows, maybe one day you'll be a famous celebrity chef, hosting cook-offs or showing how to best manage a restaurant. Or you might wind up as an executive chef, keeping an eye on several different eateries. No matter what you choose, always give it your best, and allow the rest to come in time!

My Inspiration

As a parent in this ever-changing world, it can sometimes feel overwhelming when it comes to our children's futures. New technologies seem to be arising almost every day, and with so many innovations, it creates unique professions which many of us wouldn't have dreamed to be necessary only a few years ago. Which to me is a good thing. Because with so much variety, my children can have the opportunity to pick a career that will fit their personalities and build upon their strengths. As you may imagine, this desire within me to provide my children with the resources they needed to thrive, led me to search out books that would be easy enough for them to understand while teaching them about various professions.

Shubhi Saxena
Founder, Unibino

Only, I found that these books were few and far between. Even if I could find a book about a certain profession geared towards young readers, I found them sparse inside and limited to only certain careers that may not fit my children's abilities. This is when I came up with the idea to write my own children's books, teaching them about all the various careers in the modern world. After months of researching different professions and learning more than I ever expected, I quickly realised this was going to be a bigger project than I first anticipated. I dove into the histories of these professions, discovering links to the past, and why these professions were now so important.

Ultimately my goal was to offer my children options, to show them that there is no one set path for everyone. But in this, I stumbled upon something bigger. I wanted to share this with future generations. To share with all children and parents about these careers, to help spark curiosity, and to instil a passion for the future. Everyone has special talents and abilities, and I hope that this series will be able to offer clarity and inspiration to children around the world. Because at the end of the day, it's never too early to start dreaming and never too late to take action. With this, I hope you enjoy this series and that your young ones become the best versions of themselves as they can achieve.